My First...
Baby Brother

Published in the United States by
QEB Publishing, Inc.
3 Wrigley, Suite A
Irvine, CA 92618

www.qeb-publishing.com

Library of Congress Cataloging-in-Publication Data

Marleau, Eve.
 Baby brother / by Eve Marleau ; illustrated by Michael
Garton.
    p. cm. -- (QEB my first--)
 Summary: Lizzie prepares for her role as big sister to the new
baby in the family.
 ISBN 978-1-59566-984-1 (hardcover)
 [1. Brothers and sisters--Fiction. 2. Babies--Fiction.] I.
Garton, Michael, ill. II. Title.
 PZ7.M34435Bc 2010
 [E]--dc22
                           2008056076

Author Eve Marleau
Illustrator Michael Garton
Consultants Shirley Bickler and Tracey Dils
Designer Elaine Wilkinson

Publisher Steve Evans
Creative Director Zeta Davies
Managing Editor Amanda Askew

Printed and bound in China

The words in **bold** are
explained in the glossary
on page 24.

My First...

Baby Brother

Eve Marleau and Michael Garton

QEB Publishing

Every morning, Lizzie eats her breakfast
with Mom, Dad, and Max the dog.

"Mom, how long have you been **pregnant**?"

"Nearly nine months, Lizzie. The baby will be born any day now."

"I should make some room at the table!" says Lizzie.

5

Lizzie helps Mom to wash up after breakfast.

"Where will the baby sleep, Mom?"

6

"The baby will sleep in a **cot** in my room, just like your dolly's cot. When the baby is older, he will sleep in a bed, just like you."

7

Then they take Max for
a walk in the park.

"Will the baby want
to play fetch with
Max and me?"

"The baby will
be too small to
play fetch. You
will have to wait
until he is older."

"Until then, you can spend time together in other ways. You can sing to him and tell him all about your day."

"Babies love their BIG sisters and brothers so much."

9

One day, Gran comes to
pick Lizzie up from school.

"Mom and Dad have gone to the **hospital**. It won't be long now until your baby brother arrives!"

11

Lizzie is outside in the yard with Grandad when Dad arrives.

"Dad! Dad!"

"Is my new brother here?
Where's Mom?"

"Yes, they are both at the hospital. Would you
like to come with me to meet your new brother?"

They go to the hospital to see Mom.
There is a tiny baby in
the crib next to her.

14

"Hi Lizzie. This is your brother, Charlie.
Would you like to say hello?" asks Mom.

Lizzie looks into the cot.
"I'm your BIG sister!"
she tells Charlie.

The next day, Mom
and Charlie come
home from the hospital.

16

"Can I do anything to help, Mom?" asks Lizzie.

"Yes, it's time for Charlie's bath."

Mom shows Lizzie how to make sure the bath water is just the right **temperature** for Charlie.

Then Gran and Mom put Charlie down for a sleep in his crib.

Lizzie put a blue bunny in next to him.

"This is a present from me, Charlie!" whispers Lizzie.

19

Later, Lizzie hears Charlie crying. She goes into the bedroom.

"Why is he crying, Mom?" she asks.

"Charlie is very hungry after his sleep."

"What does Charlie like to eat?" asks Lizzie.

"He only drinks special milk for the first few months. The milk has everything Charlie needs to grow."

Every morning, Lizzie likes to help Mom.

She helps to change Charlie's diaper.

She dresses him.

She plays with him.

Then they all have breakfast together at the kitchen table.

23

Glossary

Crib A baby's bed.

Diaper A piece of material that is wrapped around a baby's bottom to absorb and hold waste.

Hospital A building where people see doctors for medical treatment.

Pregnant When a woman or a female animal has a baby growing inside her.

Temperature How hot or cold something is.